Dedicated to ...

www.transworldbooks.co.uk

Dedicated to ...

The forgotten friendships, hidden stories and lost loves
found in second-hand books

W.B. GOODERHAM

BANTAM PRESS

LONDON · NEW YORK · TORONTO · SYDNEY · AUCKLAND

A Random House Group Company
www.transworldbooks.co.uk

First published in Great Britain
in 2013 by Bantam Press
an imprint of Transworld Publishers

Collection copyright © W.B. Gooderham
Individual cover copyright details listed on pages 186-189

Wayne Gooderham has asserted his right under the Copyright,
Designs and Patents Act 1988 to be identified as the author of this work.

A CIP catalogue record for this book
is available from the British Library.

ISBN 9780593072844

Addresses for Random House Group Ltd companies outside the UK
can be found at: www.randomhouse.co.uk
The Random House Group Ltd Reg. No. 954009

Printed and bound by Toppan Leefung Printing Limited, China

2 4 6 8 10 9 7 5 3 1

Dedicated to ...

James and Peter. Little readers. With love.

About the author

W B Gooderham is a freelance writer, regularly reviewing books and contributing articles on literature to the *Guardian* and *Time Out*. He lives in London and is currently writing his debut novel.

Introduction

The right book, given to the right person at the right time, can work wonders.* Spirits can be raised and horizons broadened; broken hearts can be mended, old flames rekindled, friendships reaffirmed. A book can say Sorry, and Thank You. A book can say I miss you, I love you, I forgive you; I never want to see you again.

And because reading is one of the most intimate of human activities – usually requiring silence and solitude and time – and because the interpretation of a single book will always be fluid – each reader bringing his or her own imagination, experience and emotional intelligence to bear on the text – it is not surprising that in order to share in that intimacy (albeit by proxy), or to nudge the reader towards a desired interpretation, the giver of the book will often inscribe something suitably pertinent on the flyleaf for the recipient.

As a habitual buyer of secondhand books, I came to notice that I was accidentally accruing a rather interesting sub-collection of books containing such inscriptions. These messages ranged from the awkward scratchings of adolescent infatuation, to the resentful recriminations of a love affair gone sour – and all elicited a certain frisson at reading something private, often highly personal, and patently not intended for my eyes. But I like to think that there is more to this hobby than a mere bibliophilic kink. Specifically, that

* Conversely, the wrong book given to the wrong person at the wrong time can prove disastrous.

these dedications offer tantalizing glimpses into their host books' secret histories, imbuing the physical objects with an emotional resonance quite independent of – or intriguingly linked to – the actual texts. Often the choice of book, coupled with the message within, can suggest a narrative all of its own. (Such as the copy of Jean-Paul Sartre's *Words*, addressed to 'mummy' with the instructions that she 'read it all without prejudice', including, one presumes, the cover text which baldly states, 'I loathe my childhood and all that remains of it.') Others are baffling in their incongruity. (Who would have fingered George Orwell's dystopian horror show, *Nineteen Eighty Four*, as a romantic offering? Yet here it is, crowbarred into this unlikely role by what seems to be love-giddy logic: 'This book was published in 1949, it was about the future 1984. I have given it to you with love in 1994, the start of our future.')

But, for me, the overriding emotion evoked by these inscriptions is one of pathos. At their most basic level all are records of human connections – or at least attempts at human connections – given added poignancy by the fact that all have been discovered among the shelves of secondhand book shops and, for whatever reason, are no longer in the hands of the original dedicatees.

Aside from the two aforementioned examples, and the occasional editorial note to supply context where necessary,

10

I have refrained from commenting on the dedications in this book. They should all speak for themselves – some more eloquently than others, admittedly – while the more cryptic offer plenty of scope for interpretation. (And, as a lot of the handwriting also leans towards the cryptic, most of these dedications have been transcribed for ease of reading. I apologize now for any howling misreads I may have made.)

However, I would like to briefly comment here on one dedication which I believe encapsulates the appeal of inscribing a book with a personal message. Found inside a copy of Patrick Leigh Fermor's *A Time of Gifts* is a fairly long inscription written from a son to his father, reassuring him that he need not feel obliged to read the book if it doesn't 'grab him', before going on to describe his gift, quite brilliantly, as 'a short letter with 300 pages attached'. This, surely, gets to the heart of the matter. For, while I may (grudgingly) acknowledge the practical advantages of Kindle and the like, when it comes to the giving of gifts there is still nothing to beat the physical book: a gift that not only furnishes a room, but, in a very real sense, has the potential to furnish a life, also.

W.B. Goole

A·TIME·OF
GIFTS

'...hing short of a masterpiece' – Jan Morris in the Spectator

RICK·LEIGH·FERMOR

Dear Dad,

According
the Guru of
best way to sent
Printed Matter but
include a letter. –

I enjoyed the
its sequel) a lot
was reading them,
of you, and wan
memories you have
of the times and
describes. Of cours
(of central Europe a
in 1933) vanished
you born. The mix
author's experiences of
18 and his reflections
(or any rate in 1978)
world it is impossible t
give the book an unusua
I think.

Don't feel obliged to
it doesn't "grab" you.
this as a short letter wit
attached.

Lots of love,
Seki x

P.S. Hungary is mostly in the

25/4/88

Dear Dad,

According to Mum (alias the Guru of the Postal Rates) the best way to send a book is as Printed Matter, but then it can't include a letter – hence this method.

I enjoyed this book (and its sequel) a lot. While I was reading them, I thought of you, and wondered what memories you have of any of the times and places he describes. Of course this world (of central Europe as it was in 19??) vanished before I was born. The mixture of the author's experience of it at age 18 and his reflections now (or any rate in 1978) on a world it is impossible to re-visit, give the book an unusual texture, I think.

Don't feel obliged to read it if it doesn't "grab" you. You can view this as a short letter with 300 pages attached.

Lots of Love, Satei xxx

P.S. Hungary is mostly in the second volume.

HEMINGWAY

Winner Take
Nothing

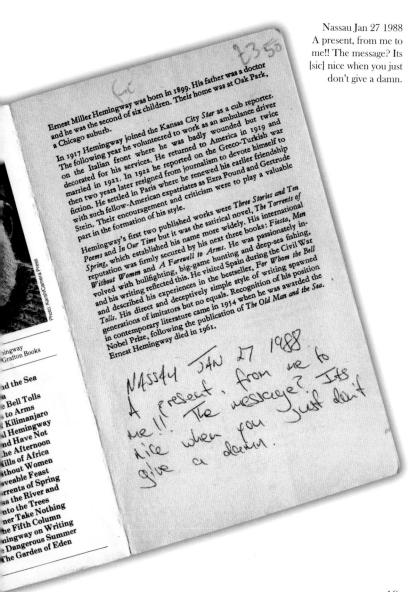

Nassau Jan 27 1988
A present, from me to
me!! The message? Its
[sic] nice when you just
don't give a damn.

Dear Kim,
I thought that visiting
your friend might get you a
bit down. Hope you enjoy
this book, it is the most
life affirming book with the
most perfect ending.
Love,
[signature]

Dear Kim,
I thought that visiting your friend might get you a bit down. Hope you enjoy
this book, it is the most life affirming book with the most perfect ending.
Love, [signature]

JOHN STEINBECK

Cannery Row

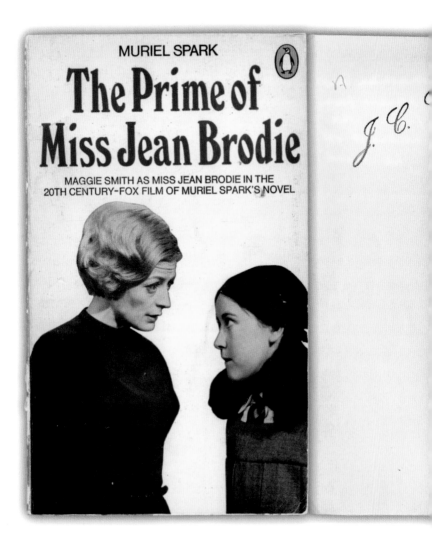

MURIEL SPARK

The Prime of Miss Jean Brodie

MAGGIE SMITH AS MISS JEAN BRODIE IN THE
20TH CENTURY-FOX FILM OF MURIEL SPARK'S NOVEL

Penguin Books
The Prime of Miss Jean Brodie

Handwritten annotations: J. Winterith / Jonathon Causer. / A kind present from / Johnny Fisher, who / nicked it off / his Aunt. / £4.50

Muriel Spark was born and educated in
Edinburgh, and spent some years in Central
Africa. She returned to Britain during the war and
worked in the Political Intelligence Department of
the Foreign Office. She subsequently edited two
poetry magazines, and her published works
include critical biographies of nineteenth-century
figures, and editions of nineteenth-century letters.
Her *Collected Poems 1* and *Collected Stories 1* were
published in 1967. Since she won an *Observer*
short-story competition in 1951 her creative
writings have achieved international recognition
(they are published in twenty different languages).
Among many other awards she has received the
Italia Prize and the James Tait Black Memorial
Prize. She was awarded the O.B.E. in 1967.

Mrs Spark became a Roman Catholic in 1954.
She has one son.

Her first novel, *The Comforters*, was published in
1957 and this was followed by *Robinson* (1958),
The Go-Away Bird and Other Stories (1958),
Memento Mori (1959), *The Ballad of Peckham Rye*
(1960), *The Bachelors* (1960), *Voices at Play* (1961),
The Prime of Miss Jean Brodie (1961), a dramatic
adaptation of which has enjoyed a long and
successful run on the West End stage. *The Girls
of Slender Means* (1963), *The Mandelbaum
Gate* (1965) and *The Public Image* (1968). Her play,
Doctors of Philosophy, was first produced in London
in 1962 and published in 1963.

Jonathon Causer.
A kind present from Johnny Fisher,
who nicked it off his Aunt.

Steal not this book for fear of shame for
here doth stand the owners name.
The Burdens – Children – Ele

Nobel Prize Winner 1970
Alexander Solzhenitsyn
One Day in the Life of
Ivan Denisovich

For darling mummy on her birthday 1971 & with lots of love and kisses from Hetty xx

PENGUIN MODERN CLASSICS

ONE DAY IN THE LIFE OF IVAN DENISOVICH

Alexander Isayevich Solzhenitsyn was born at Rostov-on-Don in 1918, the son of an office worker and a school-teacher. After graduating at Rostov University in mathematics – he took a correspondence course in literature simultaneously – he was called up for the army. He served continuously at the front as a gunner and artillery officer, was twice decorated, commanded his battery, and reached the rank of captain. In early 1945 he was arrested in an East Prussian village and charged with making derogatory remarks about Stalin. For the next eight years he was in labour camps, at first in 'general' camps along with common criminals in the Arctic and later in Beria's 'special' camps for long-term prisoners. The particular camp described in his book was in the region of Karaganda in northern Kazakhstan. Released in 1953, on Stalin's death. Solzhenitsyn had to remain in exile for three years, although his wife was allowed to join him, before returning to Russia. He settled near Ryazan and taught in a secondary school. In 1960 he submitted his novel, *One Day ...*, to Alexander Tvardovsky, the poet and editor of *Novy Mir* (New World), a literary journal; it was published, on the final decision of Khrushchev himself, in the November 1962 edition of *Novy Mir*, which sold out immediately. Two further stories by him were published during 1963. In 1968 Solzhenitsyn came under attack from the *Literary Gazette*, the Russian journal, which alleged that since 1967 his aim in life had been to oppose the basic principles of Soviet literature, and accused him of being content with the role given him by ideological enemies of Russia. He was expelled from the Soviet Writers' Union in 1970. His most recent publications are the novels *Cancer Ward* (published in Penguins) and *The First Circle*, and a play, *The Love-girl and the Innocent*.

For darling Mummy on her birthday 1971 with lots of love and kisses from Hetty xx

Sept. 73.   Bion   £3 50

PENGUIN BOOKS

WORDS

Jean-Paul Sartre – possibly the best-known and most dis-cussed modern French writer and thinker – was born in Paris in 1905. He was educated in Paris and later taught in schools at Le Havre and Laon. In 1934 he spent a year in the French Institute in Berlin where he became acquainted with modern German philosophy. He then taught at the Lycée Condorcet in Paris. He played an active role in the Resist-ance during the war, and afterwards left the teaching profes-sion. Since 1946 he has spent his time writing, and editing the magazine *Les Temps modernes*.

Sartre is a Marxist and the founder of French existential-ism. His philosophical works such as *L'Être et le néant* (1943) have had a profound effect on modern thought. His books available in Penguins are the plays *Altona*, *Men Without Shadows*, *The Flies*, *Lucifer and the Lord*, *The Respectable Prostitute*, *Kean*, *Nekrassov* and *The Trojan Women*; the novels belonging to the 'Roads to Freedom' trilogy: *The Age of Reason*, *The Reprieve* and *Iron in the Soul*; and *Nausea* (a Penguin Modern Classic).

For Mummy –
may you read it
all – clearly and
without prejudice – right
to the end!
Lots of love
Hetty xxx

Sept '73

For Mummy –
may you read it all – clearly and without prejudice – right to the end!
Lots of love,
Hetty xxx

'I loathe my
childhood
and all that
remains of it...'
Words by Jean-
Paul Sartre

7350

ANIMAL FARM

George Orwell (whose real name was Eric Blair) was born in India in 1903, and was educated at Eton. From 1922 to 1928 he served in Burma in the Indian Imperial Police. For the next two years he lived in Paris, and then came to England as a school-teacher. Later he worked in a bookshop. In 1937 he went to Spain to fight for the Republicans and was wounded. During the Second World War he was a member of the Home Guard and worked for the B.B.C. In 1943 he joined the staff of *Tribune*, contributing a regular page of political and literary commentary, *As I Please*. He later became a regular contributor to the *Observer*, for which newspaper he went as a special correspondent to France and Germany. He died in London in 1950.

His publications include *Down and Out in Paris and London*, *Burmese Days*, *The Road to Wigan Pier*, *Coming Up For Air*, *Keep the Aspidistra Flying*, and *Homage to Catalonia*. Orwell's name became widely known with the publication, in 1945, of *Animal Farm*, which has sold more than a million copies. *Nineteen Eighty-Four* had a similar success, and aroused extraordinary interest as a film and on television. *His Collected Essays, Journalism and Letters* are now available in four volumes in Penguin Books.

Weapons are the instruments
of misfortune, not of honour.
The wise man conquers
unwillingly.

Taoist.

(The First Circle,
Alexander Solshenitzin).
For Marc, from Mum. Easter 1974.

Weapons are the instruments of misfortune, not of honour.
The wise man conquers unwillingly.
Taoist
(The First Circle, Alexander Solzhenitzin [sic])
For Marc, from Mum
Easter 1974

Penguin Modern Classics

George Orwell
Animal Farm

Bawdy
Ballads

THE
WAYWARD
Enjoy BOY

**THE SEXUAL
LIFE OF
THE CAMEL**

and

I-Yi-Yi-Yi

Bawdy Ballads

Mum says it is disgusting: I say it may encourage you to learn the piano.

Mum & Dad.

Xmas 1989.

Mum says it is disgusting: I say it may encourage you to learn the piano.
Mum & Dad, Xmas 1989

DOVER · THRIFT · EDI

shakespear

MUCH AD
ABOUT NOTH

April 15th 2006.

Our story . . .
[It is a beautiful, sunny, Southern California day,
Robert & Marie-Hélène are walking to the grocery store]

She said: Let's get married!
He said: [pause] Sure.
She said: REALLY?
He said: Yes, really.
She said: Seriously?
He said: Yup. Let's have a small, simple wedding
She said: Okay. OK. K. As long as we invite Kim and Paul!

Robert Marie-Hélène

April 15th 2006   *£1*

iR073

DOVER · THRIFT · EDITIONS

Our story...

Much Ado About Nothing

WILLIAM SHAKESPEARE

[It is a beautiful, sunny, Southern California day. Robert & Marie-Hélène are walking to the grocery store].

She said: Let's get married!

He said: [Pause]. Sure.

She said: REALLY?

He said: Yes, really.

She said: Seriously?

He said: Yup. Let's have a small, simple wedding.

She said: Okay. OK. k. As long as we invite Kim and Paul!

DOVER PUBLICATIONS, INC.
New York

Robert   *Marie-Hélène*

The greatest true story
of escape and adventure
ever written!

U.K. CANADA $3.00
AUSTRALIA $2.35 NEW ZEALAND $2.75

AUTOBIOGRAPHY
586 03486 2

PAPILLON

HENRI CHARRIÈRE

PAPILLON
HENRI CHARRIÈRE

Panther
586 03486 2

THE GREATEST TRUE STORY OF ESCAPE AND ADVENTURE EVER WRITTEN

Condemned for a murder he had not committed, Henri Charrière (nicknamed Papillon) was sent to the penal colony of French Guiana. Forty-two days after his arrival he made his first break, travelling a thousand gruelling miles in an open boat. Recaptured, he suffered solitary confinement and was sent eventually to Devil's Island, a hell-hole of disease and brutality. No one had ever escaped from this notorious prison – no one until Papillon took to the shark-infested sea supported only by a makeshift coconut-sack raft. In thirteen years he made nine daring escapes, living through many fantastic adventures while on the run – including a sojourn with South American Indians whose women Papillon found welcomely free of European restraints ...
PAPILLON is filled with tension, adventure and high excitement. It is also one of the most vivid stories of human endurance ever written.

* Top of the bestseller lists all over the world
*Film rights sold for over $500,000
*American Book-of-the-Month Club selection

THE BOOK THAT TOOK THE WORLD BY STORM

*Happy Valentines my love,
This is not a text book of
how to get out of the wedding!
(see back)
All my love,
Ben 14/2/76*

Happy Valentine's my love,
This is not a text book of how to get out of the wedding! (see back)
All my love,
Ben 14/2/76

To my dearest Sonia
We've had our own 1,000 and
1 nights of marriage - more
or less. Three years already!
I still discover things about
you I love each day, or
rediscover: your constancy,
your generosity, your sense of
justice. I count myself a
happy man to have found
you, and I hope it lasts
as many years as we can count.
I love you; Tom.

To my dearest Sonia

We've had our own 1,000 and 1 nights of marriage – more or less. Three years already! I still discover things about you I love each day, or rediscover: your constancy, your generosity, your sense of justice. I count myself a happy man to have found you, and I hope it lasts as many years as we can count.

I love you, Tom

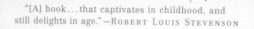

"[A] book...that captivates in childhood, and
still delights in age." —ROBERT LOUIS STEVENSON

THE ARABIAN NIGHTS

TALES FROM
A THOUSAND AND ONE NIGHTS

Translated, with a Preface and Notes, by
SIR RICHARD F. BURTON

Introduction by A. S. BYATT

5TZ, England
ew York 10014, USA
a, Australia
ario, Canada M4V 3B2
nd 10, New Zealand

Middlesex, England

n Brook, 1994

n of this copyright page

erted

plc

For Maria

FoR Rebecca

In case you have any ideas!

For Rebecca
In case you have any ideas!

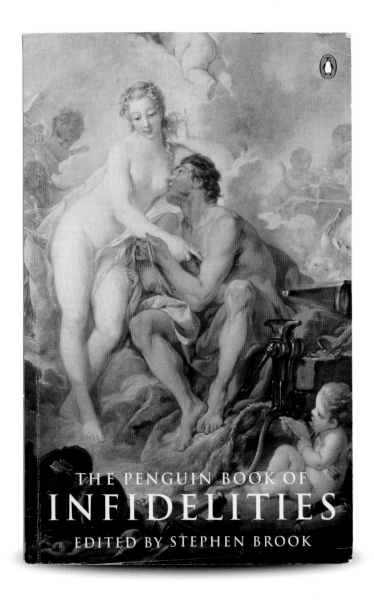

THE PENGUIN BOOK OF
INFIDELITIES

EDITED BY STEPHEN BROOK

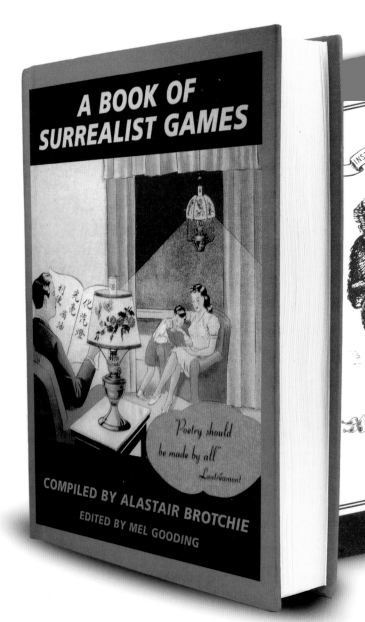

A BOOK OF SURREALIST GAMES

"Poetry should be made by all"
Lautréamont

COMPILED BY ALASTAIR BROTCHIE
EDITED BY MEL GOODING

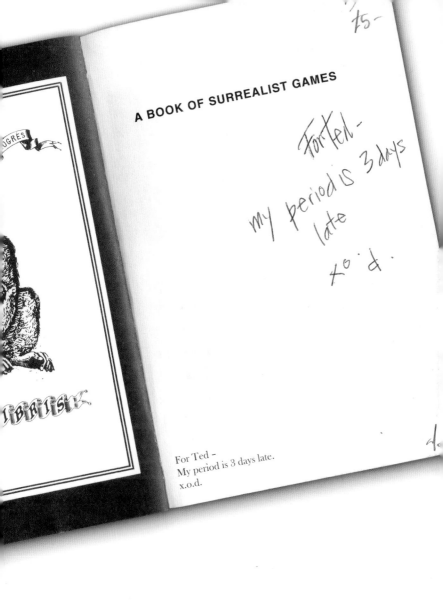

A BOOK OF SURREALIST GAMES

For Ted -
My period is 3 days late.
x.o.d.

Dec 21st 08

– I love you –

To my darling Husband –
We have now been married for 6 very special months.
Enjoy memories of our wonderful Honeymoon as
you read this.
Anita xxx

I love you

Dec 21st 08

Agatha Christie

Death on the Nile

To my darling
Husband -
We have now
been married
for 6 very special
months.
Enjoy memories
of our wonderful
Honeymoon as
you read
this

HARPER

Anita xxx

Aharon Shabtai

J'Accuse

AWARD FOR POETRY IN TRANSLATION
PEN
2004

Translated from the Hebrew by Peter Cole

Summer has co[...]
the grass on the hill wit[...]
Look at the shoemaker, ther[...]
the scrawl across his brow [...]
that the wells of morality [...]
Now sweaty rubber sole[...]
yes, the flies for which [...]
swarm by swarm wil[...]
Thank God that I, a[...]
can bend my back

[...]e
[...]th[...]
[...]r wit[...]
[...]them.
[...]d more [...]
[...]e waters [...]
[...]only when [...]

28th September 2006
My friend –
I send you this gift, which is self-explanatory, and hope you'll find the poet's work more accessible than my obscure efforts to say same similar things. When I found the book last week, I wanted to tell you about it, because it is to you that I have been addressing my thoughts. I enclose a sprig of mint as an emblem of faith that you will visit and drink mint tea with me again sometime – I hope before too long, when I am less hurt, and less vulnerable, and better able to accept what you can offer.
Until then –
with enormous affection and care for you, my dear –
Jasmine.

ne dry, the w
ce, and the flies,
no rep   ch,   f my hairless pate.
sit on
et, fift
yself i

28th September 2006

My friend —
I send you this gift, which is
self-explanatory, and hope you'll
find the poet's work more accessible
than my obscure efforts to say
some similar things. When I
found the book last week I wanted
to tell you about it, because it is
to you that I have been addressing my thoughts.
I enclose a sprig of mint as an emblem
of faith that you will visit and
drink mint tea with me again
sometime — I hope before too long,
when I am less hurt, and less
vulnerable, and better able to
accept what you can offer.

Until then —
with enormous affection and
care for you, my dear —

Jasmine

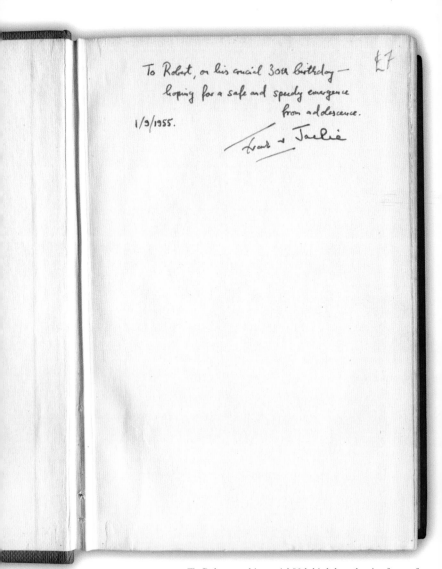

To Robert, on his crucial 30th birthday – hoping for a safe
and speedy emergence from adolescence.
Frank & Jackie
1/9/1955

£7

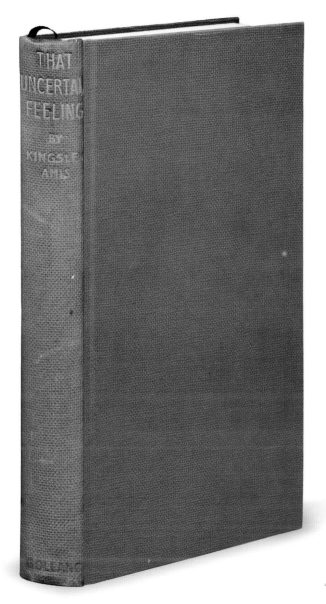

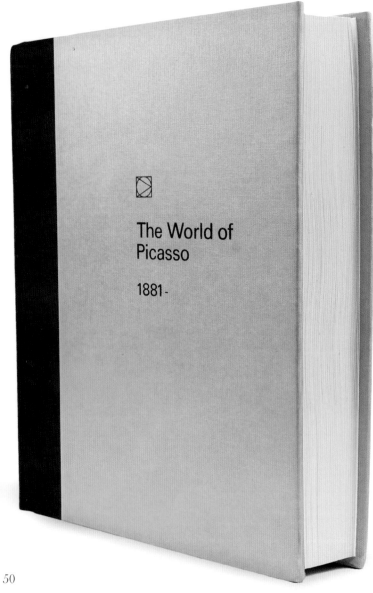

The World of
Picasso

1881 -

The one thing one can always do for the person one has loved – <u>IS</u> love them again.
I'm so glad – that way I <u>can</u> <u>do</u> anything for you, include giving you this book –
[signature] 30/3/71

A
HAIKU GARDEN

THE FOUR SEASONS IN POEMS
AND PRINTS

By Stephen Addiss
with Fumiko and Akira Yamamoto

Gladiksia — Ruby lace shining
Fallen leaves tomorrow

Carol,
1998

Gladiksia —
Ruby Lace shining
Fallen leaves tomorrow
キャロル・アービン
CAROL. 1998.

When the written word appears before us in its simplicity - then we see that in the joy of expression we may have lost the honesty of thought which alone makes writing worth while. There is no right or wrong way - the choice is between two terrible wrongs and the most gifted and well-informed people will hesitate before coming down on either side. The events of the next few days might help us to decide - in the meantime prayer and honest desire to do God's will are the only things left to us.

SELECTED MODERN SHORT STORIES

H. E. BATES
MARTIN ARMSTRONG
H. A. MANHOOD
T. O. BEACHCROFT
HELEN SIMPSON
JOHN HAMPSON

LIAM O'FLAHERTY
L. A. G. STRONG
MALACHI WHIT
FRANK O'CON
WILLIAM PLO
RHYS DAVIE

SELECTION BY ALAN STEELE

Front Flyleaf

When the written word appears before us in its simplicity – then we see that in the joy
of expression we may have lost the honesty of thought which alone makes writing worth
while. There is no right or wrong way – the choice is between two terrible wrongs and
the most gifted and well informed people will hesitate before coming down on either
side. The events of the next few days might help us to decide – in the meantime
prayer and honest desire to do God's will are the only things left to us.

Back Flyleaf

September 26th 1938.

The chief emotions today are great anxiety, fear, spiritual loneliness. Of actual
physical danger there is very little fear; men are prepared to sacrifice themselves
for something which they believe is greater than themselves. For many people,
the greatest fear is that this civilisation which in spite of all its differences,
embraces so much loveliness and embodies the hopes and dreams of so many
individuals, shall be swept away and that in its place we may see a mechanically
perfect but soulless and inhuman Godless society.

[See author note p185]

To my darling Rose,

    I once read this in a novel about Chinese life: "Success. What is it? A bubble that breaks at the touch. A shallow dream that too often ends in bitterness and despair. The only kind of success is the peace that can come from one's own heart, the ability to live with one's own self and not be ashamed, to love one good woman and with her taste life to its very dregs. That is success and the only kind worth having."

    Together, we shall, please God, make a success of our lives.

            With all my love,

                Aron.

חוונה גת תש"ו.
November 1945.

To my darling Rose,

I once read this in a novel about Chinese life: "Success. What is it? A bubble that breaks at the touch. A shallow dream that too often ends in bitterness and despair. The only kind of success is the peace that can come from one's own heart, the ability to live with one's own self and not be ashamed, to love one good woman and with her taste life to its very dregs. That is success and the only kind worth having."

Together, we shall, please God, make a success of our lives.

With all my love, Aron.

[In Hebrew] Kislev, 5706
November 1945

To Phyll.

Xmas 1921.

"The Thousandth Man is worth them all."

Kipling.

To Phyll, Xmas 1921.
"The Thousandth Man is worth them all"
Kipling

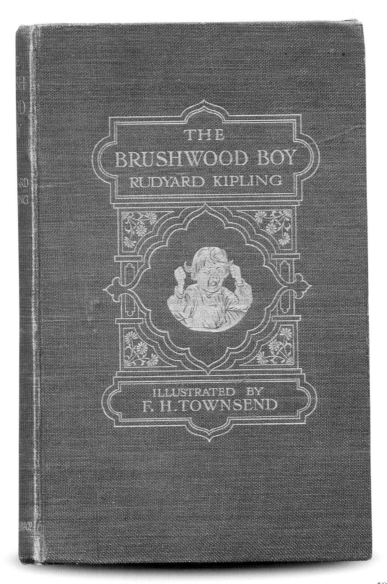

THE
BRUSHWOOD BOY
RUDYARD KIPLING

ILLUSTRATED BY
F. H. TOWNSEND

SYLVIA PLATH

Ariel

To Edie
Happy 60th Birthday
with love

Gill

" Ariel is the spirit of poetry, the
embodiment of inspiration and
genius."

The ariel voice is plangent with
griefs and beauties and I hope you
enjoy the essence that is Sylvie Platt
at her height.

To Edie
Happy 60th Birthday
With love
Gill

"Ariel is the spirit of poetry,
the embodiment of inspiration
and genius."

The ariel voice is plangent
with griefs and beauties and
I hope you enjoy the essence
that is Sylvia Plath at her
height.

THE SOVEREIGN SUN

*Since I cannot wrap up
the sunshine
here are the poems
that always made it happen
for me.*

Just like you do.

*Happy birthday.
Vicky*

Since I cannot wrap up the sunshine here are the
poems that always made it happen for me.

Just like you do.

Happy Birthday
Vicky

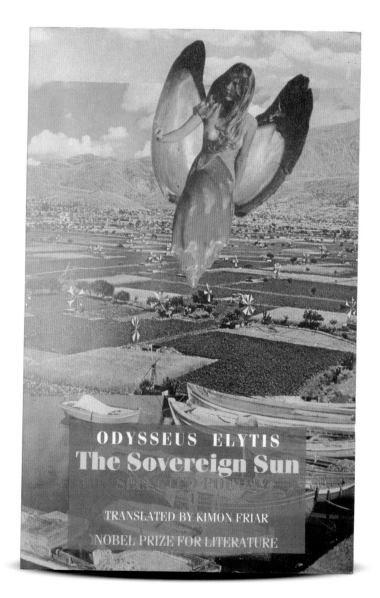

ODYSSEUS ELYTIS

The Sovereign Sun

SELECTED POEMS

TRANSLATED BY KIMON FRIAR

NOBEL PRIZE FOR LITERATURE

The Tao
of Pooh
&
The Te
of Piglet

BENJAMIN
HOFF

The Tao
of Pooh
of Pooh
&
The Te
of Piglet

&

The Te
of Piglet

德

methuen

BENJAMIN HOFF

My Darling Christopher,
 I Love you with everything
I have and everything I am.
You are my night and day,
my sun and stars. I never
have to be anything but
myself with you and that
means the world to me. I
cant wait to spend the
rest of my life with you

All of my All

Charlotte

x

Penguin ⬡ Classics

LANGLAND

(P)IERS THE PLOUGHMAN

"I wil worschip ther-with : Tr...
And ben his pilgryme att...
for pore m...

B-text VI, 103.

Godbless you in...
Peter. I hope y...
to read (orre-
that it prou...
as I have

Plea...
(a...

Than...
wis...

THE PENGUIN CL...
FOUNDER EDITOR (1944–64): E...

Editor: Betty Radice

"I wil worship ther-with: Treuth, bi my lyve, and ben
his pilgryme atte plowe: for pore mennes sake."
B-text VI, 103.

God bless you in your retirement, Peter. I hope you
can find time to read (or re-read?) this, and that it
proves to be as inspiring as I have found it.

Piers (and family!)

Thank you for your wisdom.

To Ruth:
"I was a stranger and
you welcomed me."
          Thank you for making me
think about the "O" in God.
          Let's keep going –

4.4.08
Ireland

[handwritten signature]

4.4.08
Ireland

To Ruth:
"I was a stranger and you welcomed me."
Thank you for making me think about the "O" in God.
Let's keep going –
[Signature]

68

BLACKBIRD
AND WOLF

POEMS BY HENRI COLE

Letter to a Christian Nation

SAM HARRIS

AUTHOR OF
THE END OF FAITH

To ~~Christian~~ Christine,

Merry Christmas !!!

I'm not forcing you into anything yea, just want you to start thinking ↗ [goofy-faced doodle]

Enjoy da book . . . . . .

[signature]

To ~~Christian~~ Christine,
Merry Christmas!!!
I'm not forcing you into anything yea, just want you to
start thinking [goofy-faced doodle]
Enjoy da book . . .
[signature]

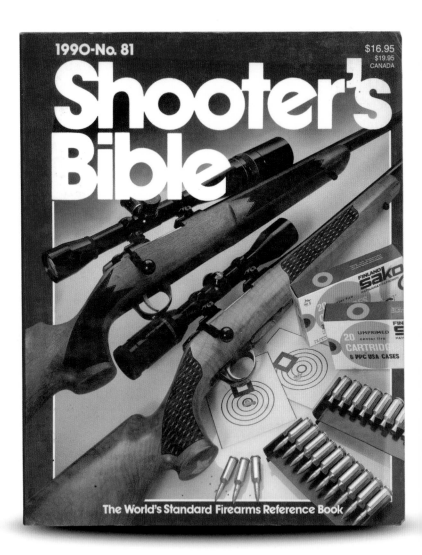

1990-No. 81

$16.95
$19.95
CANADA

Shooter's Bible

The World's Standard Firearms Reference Book

To Matt, From Daniel . . .
"Happy Hunting!"

"One day a
real rain
will come,
and wash
all the scum
off the streets . . ."
Taxi Driver

28·72·

ABOUT OUR COVER

The two scoped Sako rifles featured on our front cover this year are the PPC Benchrest/Varmint (top) and the PPC Deluxe (bottom). The cartridges illustrated represent factory-loaded ammunition and factory unprimed brass produced by Sako at the company's plant in Finland. Since their introduction, these components have together set virtually every world record in national and international benchrest competition. Now, they are fast becoming popular among small-game and varmint hunters as well. Readers who would like to know more about the PPC story are invited to read Will Pyle's interesting and informative article, "The 6 PPC: From Shooting Range to Hunting Field," which begins on page 26.

To Matt, From Daniel . . . Happy Hunting!
"One day a real rain will come and wash all the scum off the streets . . ."
Taxi Driver 23.72

Shooter's Bible

To Tony Letters   16 January 89
        Miller is my friend, my   o/o 88
father, my lover ; not a God,
because that would be in
the realms of metaphysics'
and unattainable. He is the
Rose (thorns included) in my crucifixion.

                        Garry.

16 January 89

To Tony,
Miller is my friend, my father, my lover; not a God, because that
would be in the realms of metaphysics and unattainable.
He is the Rose (thorns included) in my crucifixion.
Garry.

The Ballad of Reading Gaol

May 2005

For Mo,

Sometimes 'only when it is
dark can you see the stars'.

With love,
Claudia.

with woodcuts by Frans Masereel

The BALLAD of READING GAOL

OSCAR WILDE

journeyman

ANGELA CARTER

Wise Children

18.5.93.

Bridget,
   you often have to travel far from
the self in order to truly find yourself.
Your journey to these alien lands is
underway now. So go out there searching
for the truth and return enriched.
    You have an immense amount of talent;
don't ever let anyone tell you otherwise.
    happy travelling,
        love
          Phil.

18.5.93

Bridget,

You often have to travel far from the self in order to truly find yourself. Your journey to these alien lands is underway now. So go out there searching for the truth and return enriched. You have an immense amount of talent; don't ever let anyone tell you otherwise. Happy travelling, Love Phil.

06/10
v

New £10-
£5-

NEHRU

Dear George,
      Congratulations on turning
25! A number significant not
just in cricket, but also in Indian
philosophy as it denotes the phase in
one's life when one passes from the ~~gria~~-
brahmacharya ashram to the ~~hastha~~ ashram. That is to say from
the supposedly austere, disciplined and
celibate life of a student to the
dutiful life of a 'householder' - fulfilling
his duties to his spouse, children, aged
parents and the community!
      Wishing you a very Happy Birthday.
      Warm regards,

          Jubin.

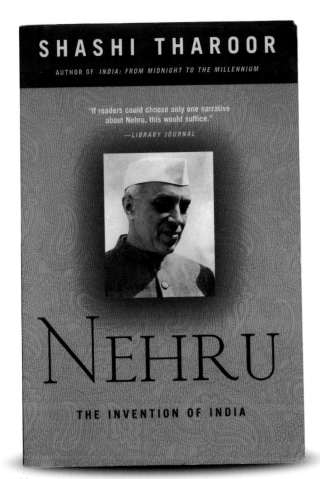

8th June 2006

Dear George,

Congratulations on turning 25! A number significant not just in cricket, but also in Indian philosophy as it denotes the phase in one's life when one passes from the brahmacharya ashram to the gri-hastha ashram. That is to say from the supposedly austere, disciplined and celibate life of a student to the dutiful life of 'householder' – fulfilling his duties to his spouse, children, aged parents and the community!

Wishing you a very Happy Birthday.

Warm regards,

Julian

a Penguin Book

5/-

I, Claudius

Robert Graves

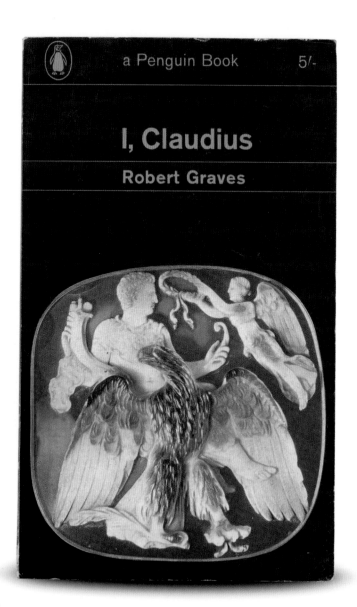

July '66'

To John

From Jim who
intends to star
in 'The Epic that
will be'. For you,
I hope this book
will give you
tremendous pleasure

July '66

To John

From Jim who intends to star in 'The Epic that will be'. For you,
I hope this book will give you tremendous pleasure

Sulaiman,

When the year first started out, I was so convinced that you didn't like me. After a little time (and some baking), you've become one of my most reliable people here. I have so much respect for you - whip-smart, funny, loyal - stay awesome, okay? Thank you for being a part of my family here this year. I'm going to miss you, but I can't wait to hear about all the fantastic things you'll be doing, next year and beyond. I know everything you'll be doing just spectacular for you. Whenever we're in the same city again, remember you've got a girl to bake for you.

♡ Stephanie

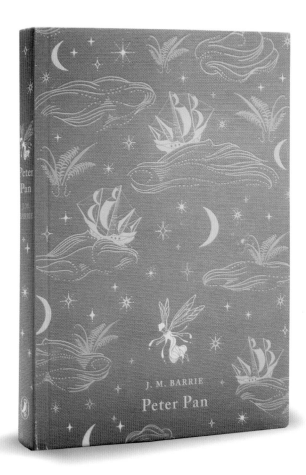

Sulaiman,

When the year first started out, I was so convinced that you didn't like me. After a little time (and some baking), you've become one of my most reliable people here. I have so much respect for you – whip-smart, funny, loyal – stay awesome, okay? Thank you for being a part of my family here this year. I'm going to miss you, but I can't wait to hear about all the fantastic things you'll be doing, next year and beyond. I know everything will be just spectacular for you. Whenever we're in the same city again, remember you've got a girl to bake for you!

Stephanie

[See author note p185]

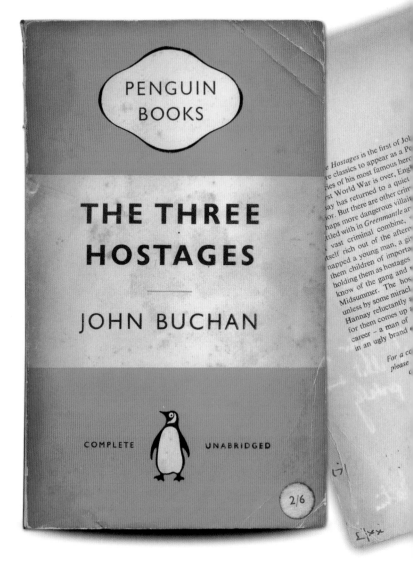

PENGUIN
BOOKS

THE THREE
HOSTAGES

JOHN BUCHAN

COMPLETE   UNABRIDGED

2/6

...e Hostages is the first of Joh
...e classics to appear as a Pe
...ries of his most famous hero
...rst World War is over, Eng
...ay has returned to a quiet
...or. But there are other crim
...haps more dangerous villain
...tled with in *Greenmantle* an
... vast criminal combine.
...itself rich out of the afterw
...napped a young man, a gi
...them children of importan
...holding them as hostages
...know of the gang and u
...Midsummer. The hos
...unless by some mirac
...Hannay reluctantly
...for them comes up
...career – a man of
...in an ugly brand

*For a co
please*

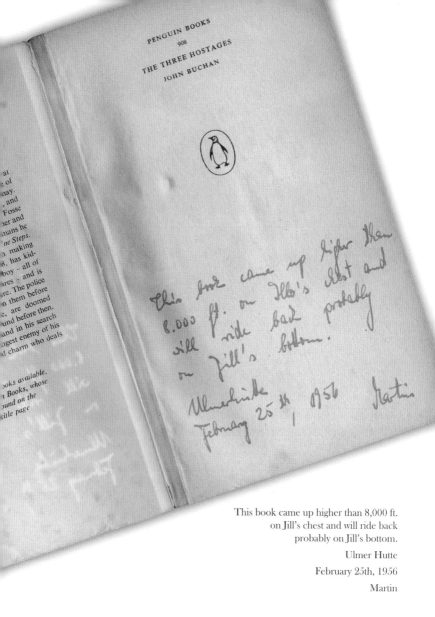

PENGUIN BOOKS

908

THE THREE HOSTAGES

JOHN BUCHAN

This book came up higher than 8,000 ft.
on Jill's chest and will ride back
probably on Jill's bottom.

Ulmer Hutte

February 25th, 1956

Martin

87

JEROME K. JEROME

THREE MEN IN A BOAT

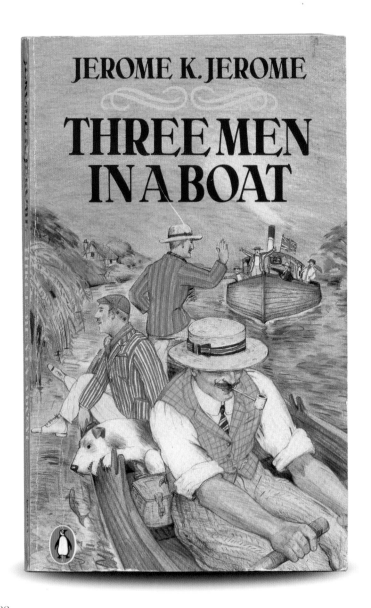

5/9/94

Richard, I've been looking for this book, since the walk and have only just found it.
I thought it might give you some inspiration for the next jolly caper! (Goretex out, striped blazers in)
Thanks for putting so much effort into organising the walk. The whole weekend most entertaining, not to say challenging.

Cheers, Paul.

5/9/94

Richard, I've been looking for this book, since the walk and have only just found it. I thought it might give you some inspiration for the next jolly caper! (Goretex out, striped blazers in) Thanks for putting so much effort into organising the walk. The whole weekend was most entertaining, not to say challenging.

Cheers,

Paul

DECLINE AND FALL

EvelynWaugh

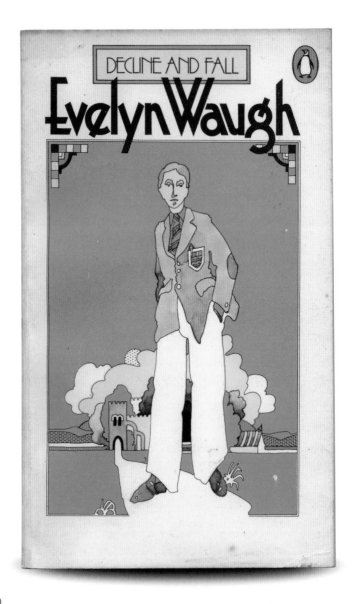

7 December 1988

To my friend Andrew,
"who could be trusted to see to luggage at foreign railway-stations and might be expected to acquit himself with decision and decorum in all the emergencies of civilized life"

Fondly,

Jane Smettells

---

7 December 1988
To my friend Andrew,
"who could be trusted to see to luggage at foreign railway-stations and might be expected to acquit himself with decision and decorum in all the emergencies of civilized life".
Fondly,
Jane [Signature]

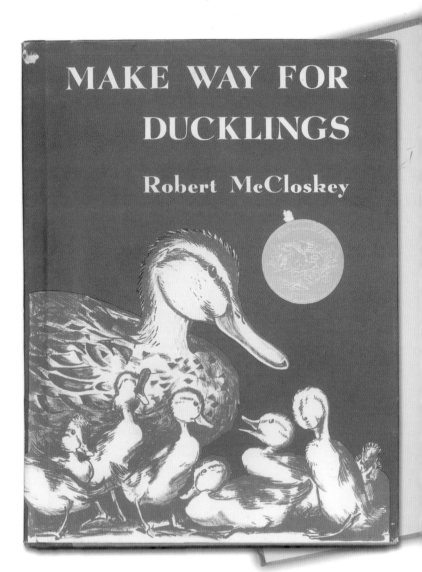

MAKE WAY FOR
DUCKLINGS

Robert McCloskey

Michael,
I want to thank you for welcoming me into your community. The time that I have spent at West London will truly be my fondest memories of my semester here in London. I hope you and Olga will enjoy this story with Samuel as I enjoyed it growing up in Boston.
You always have a friend on my side of the ocean.
— Shoshana Weiner.

April 1985

To Mike,

With best wishes for the future and thanks for the recent past. Hope it won't be too long before we meet again.

Gary.

April 1985.
To Mike,
With best wishes for the future and thanks for the recent past.
Hope it won't be too long before we meet again.
Gary

The Last
TESTAMENT
of
OSCAR
WILDE

'Absolutely stunning'
THE TIMES

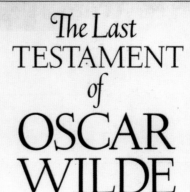

Peter Ackroyd

Judy Blume

FOREVER

Dear Claire
This has got to be
a teenage classic!

So to a 40 year old
from another heres
to forever being
a teen.

♡ much love

PAN Nat.

XXX

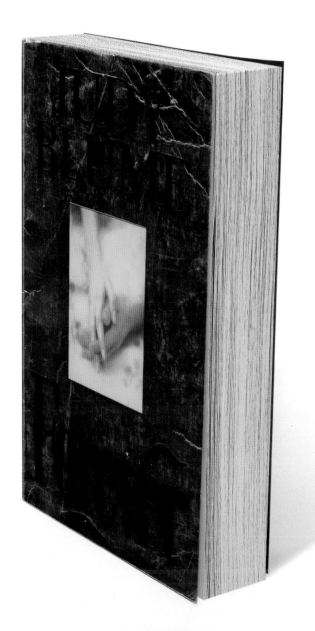

3s 6d

THE COLD EMBRACE

Stories of the macabre
Edited by Alex Hamilton

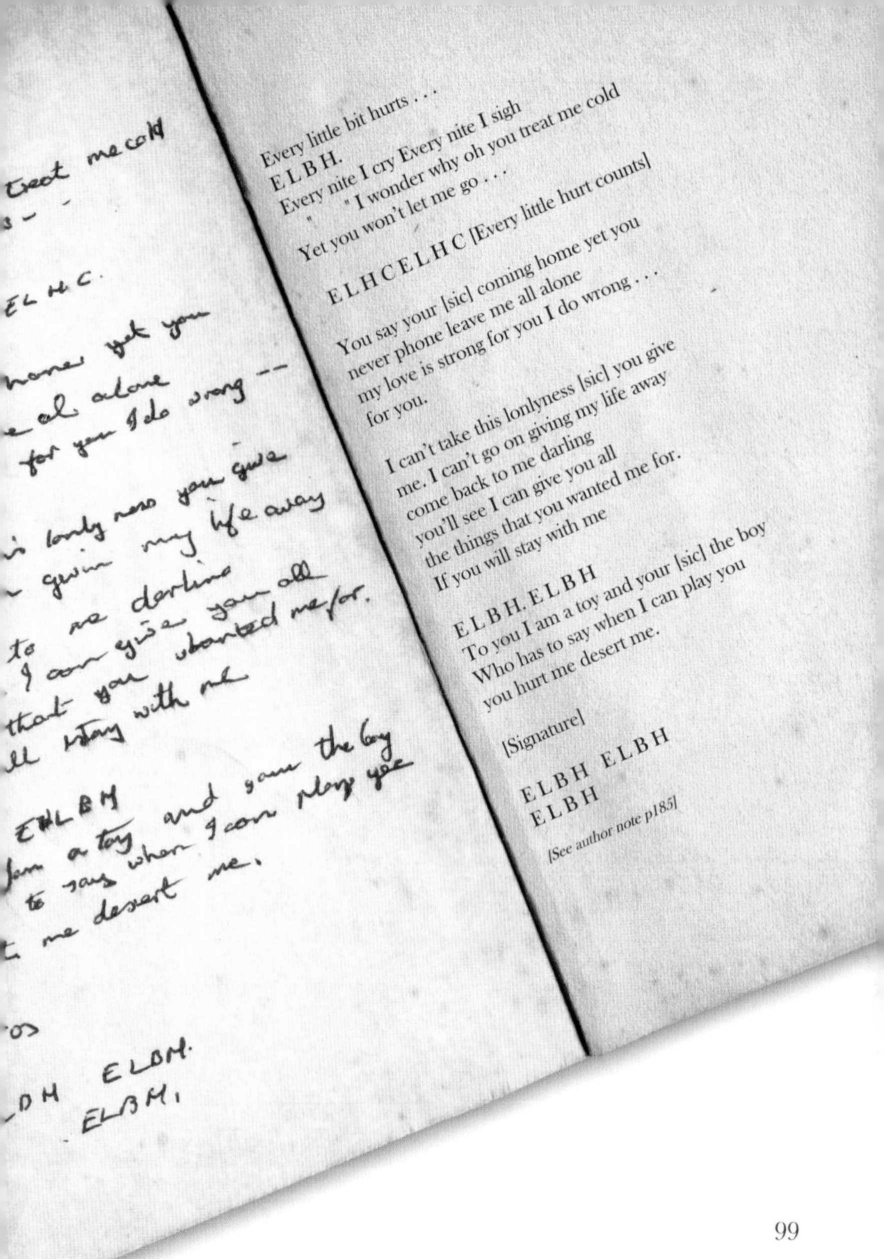

treat me cold
s - .

E L H C.

home yet you
e al alone
for you I do wrong --

s lonlyness you give
~ givin my life away
to me darling
I can give you all
that you wanted me for.
ll stay with me

E H L B H
I am a toy and sam the boy
to says when I can play you
t me desert me.

os

DH ELBH.
ELBH.

<!-- Right page (typed) -->
Every little bit hurts . . .
E L B H.
Every nite I cry Every nite I sigh
"   " I wonder why oh you treat me cold
Yet you won't let me go . . .

E L H C E L H C [Every little hurt counts]

You say your [sic] coming home yet you
never phone leave me all alone
my love is strong for you I do wrong . . .
for you.

I can't take this lonlyness [sic] you give
me. I can't go on giving my life away
come back to me darling
you'll see I can give you all
the things that you wanted me for.
If you will stay with me

E L B H . E L B H
To you I am a toy and your [sic] the boy
Who has to say when I can play you
you hurt me desert me.

[Signature]

E L B H   E L B H
E L B H

[See author note p185]

99

"My dear Cousin Elizabeth,"

I couldn't bear the thought of your having missed out on this section of the exam. Hope you enjoy it !!

love,

Alsop

WORDSWORTH CLASSICS

JANE AUSTEN

Pride
and
Prejudice

F. SCOTT FITZGERALD

The Beautiful and Damned

Dearest Kathryn

. . . Wherever you are reading this and however you are . . . I think of you.

Enjoy my favourite book.

Dearest love

[Signature] xxx

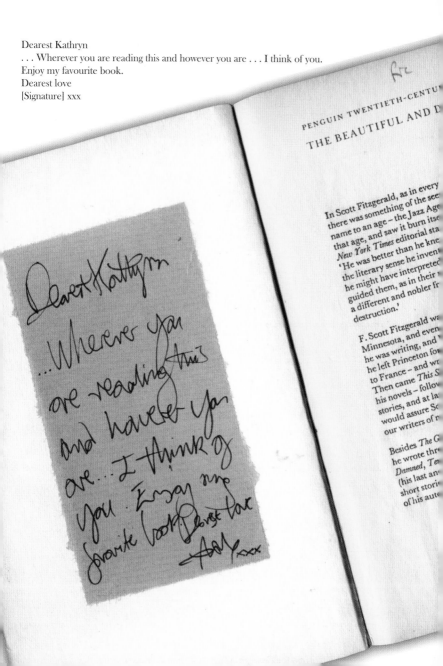

In Scott Fitzgerald, as in every
there was something of the see
name to an age – the Jazz Age
that age, and saw it burn itse
New York Times editorial sta
'He was better than he kne
the literary sense he inven
he might have interpreted
guided them, as in their
a different and nobler fr
destruction.'

F. Scott Fitzgerald wa
Minnesota, and even
he was writing, and
he left Princeton for
to France – and wr
Then came *This S*
his novels – follow
stories, and at la
would assure So
our writers of r

Besides *The G*
he wrote thr
Damned, Te
(his last an
short storie
of his aute

A Severed Head

Iris Murdoch

[Handwritten note on facing page:]

Far too sophisticated for
me I suppose is the
answer.
Yet I can read it. In
a strange way it
compels me.
I don't find it at all
funny but can see
that as a play I
could be fabulously
funny.
I think the characters
are revolting. It
makes me even more
sick to think that
it's been written
by a woman. Ugh!

I'm quite bewildered
by it.

A Se

IRIS

PEN

in association

Far too sophisticated for me I suppose is the answer.
Yet I can read it. In a strange way it compels me.
I don't find it at all funny but can see that as a play it could be fabulously funny.
I think the characters are revolting. It makes me even more sick to think that it's been written by a woman. Ugh!
I'm quite bewildered by it.

For Paul

50 PEOPLE WHO
BUGGERED UP BRITAIN

→ I ~~know~~ you won't
be the 51st!!.
The very best of
luck with the
business.

David.

10 May 2010

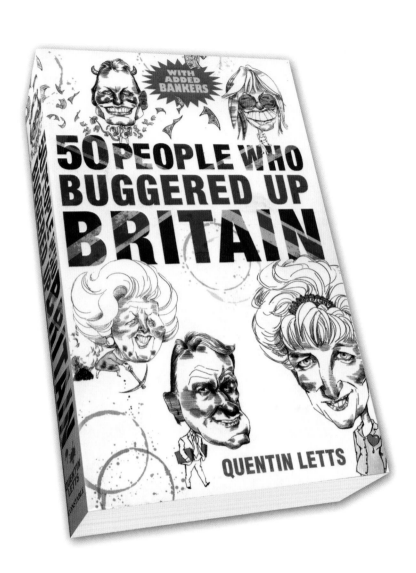

WITH
ADDED
BANKERS

50 PEOPLE WHO
BUGGERED UP
BRITAIN

QUENTIN LETTS

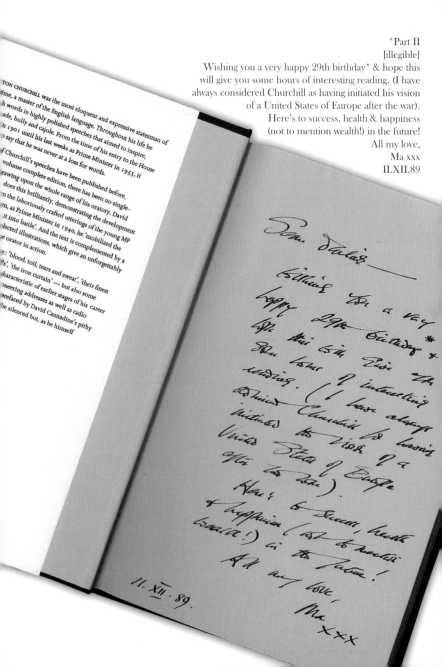

*Part II
[illegible]
Wishing you a very happy 29th birthday* & hope this
will give you some hours of interesting reading. (I have
always considered Churchill as having initiated his vision
of a United States of Europe after the war).
Here's to success, health & happiness
(not to mention wealth!) in the future!
All my love,
Ma xxx
II.XII.89

TON CHURCHILL was the most eloquent and expressive statesman of
me, a master of the English language. Throughout his life he
h words in highly polished speeches that aimed to inspire,
ade, bully and cajole. From the time of his entry to the House
n 1901 until his last weeks as Prime Minister in 1955, it
o say that he was never at a loss for words.

f Churchill's speeches have been published before,
volume complete edition, there has been no single-
rawing upon the whole range of his oratory. David
does this brilliantly, demonstrating the development
m the laboriously crafted utterings of the young
en, as Prime Minister in 1940, he 'mobilized the
it into battle'. And the text is complemented by a
lected illustrations, which give an unforgettably
e orator in action.

e : 'blood, toil, tears and sweat', their finest
s', 'the iron curtain' — but also some
haracteristic of earlier stages of his career
oneering addresses as well as radio
refaced by David Cannadine's pithy
e silenced but, as he himself

[handwritten note, right page:]

Dear Darling —

Wishing you a very
happy 29th birthday *
& hope this will give the
some hours of interesting
reading. (I have always
considered Churchill as having
initiated his vision of a
United States of Europe
after the war).

Here's to success, health
& happiness (not to mention
wealth!) in the future!

All my love,
Ma
xxx

11. XII. 89.

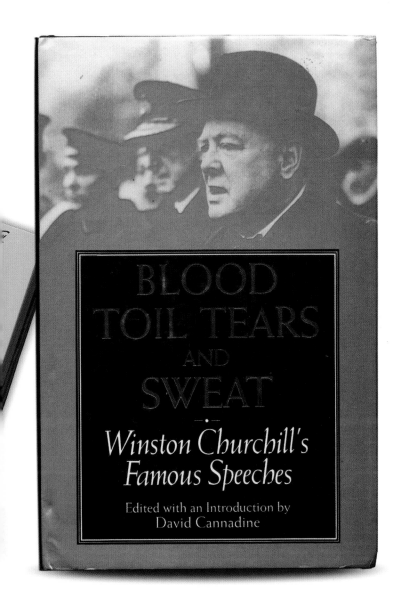

BLOOD
TOIL TEARS
AND
SWEAT

Winston Churchill's
Famous Speeches

Edited with an Introduction by
David Cannadine

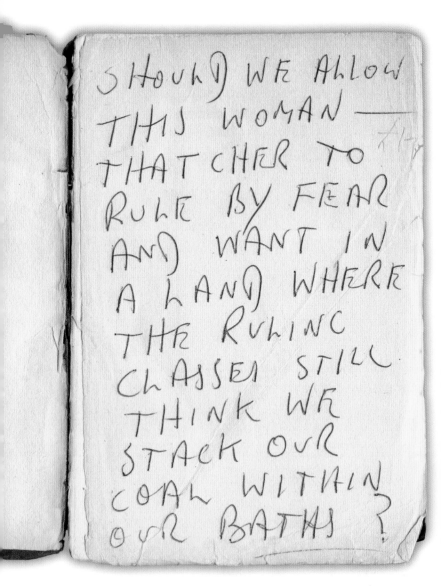

SHOULD WE ALLOW
THIS WOMAN —
THATCHER TO
RULE BY FEAR
AND WANT IN
A LAND WHERE
THE RULING
CLASSES STILL
THINK WE
STACK OUR
COAL WITHIN
OUR BATHS?

Should we allow this woman – Thatcher to rule by fear and want in a land where the ruling classes still think we stack our coal within our baths?

SWARTHMORE LECTURE   51716

UNEMPLOYMENT
AND PLENTY

57916

SHIPLEY N. BRAYSHAW, M.I.Mech.E.

VIRGINIA WOOLF

THREE GUINEAS
FIRST PAPERBACK EDITION

Hilary

Happy Christmas

love and liberation

from Paul x

You satisfied my hunger,
[Signature] 8/21/75

LOVE GODDESSES
of the Movies

Roger Manvell

To Carol

The Play we liked

~~Happy~~ Christmas

Love

Peter

Dec '93

EURIPIDES

MEDEA

TRANSLATED BY

ALISTAIR ELLIOT

INTRODUCTION BY

NICHOLAS DROMGOOLE

fear is very frightening but
when you can over the weeks,
months ahead listen to her and
see her friend.

OBERON BOOKS

Euripides

translated by Alistair Elliot

MEDEA

To Carol
The play we liked, Happy Christmas,
Love Peter, Dec '93

Fear is very frightening but when you can over the
weeks, months ahead listen to her and be her friend.

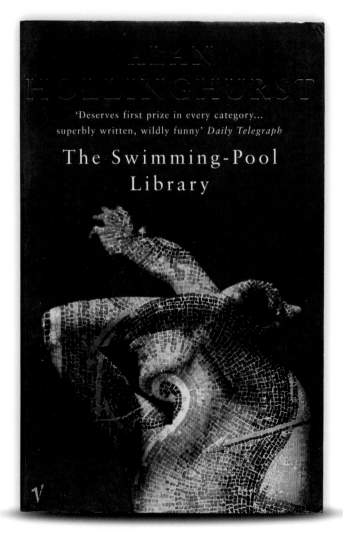

ALAN
HOLLINGHURST

'Deserves first prize in every category...
superbly written, wildly funny' *Daily Telegraph*

The Swimming-Pool Library

Dear Gengiz,
Known as [Festeklan Jahchesy] From now on you've got my blissing [sic] dear, so
NO FEAR. ON ON HAVE the best of ALL.

Amy [Signature]

THE SWIMMING-POOL LIBRARY

Alan Hollinghurst was born in 1954. He is the author of one of the most highly praised first novels to appear in the 1980s, *The Swimming-Pool Library* (1988), and was selected as one of the Best of Young British Novelists 1993. His second novel, *The Folding Star*, won the James Tait Black Memorial Prize and was shortlisted for the 1994 Booker Prize. He was on the staff of the *Times Literary Supplement* from 1982 to 1995.

£4.50

Dear Gengiz,
Known as [Festeklan Bahchesy]

From now on you've got my blissing dear. so No FEAR. ON ON HAVE The best of All.

ANY Yemeyian

The Films of
Marilyn Monroe

Edited by Michael Conway and Mark Ricci
with a tribute by Lee Strasberg
and an introduction by Mark Harris

John Stephen 1965

My Darling Margot,
Love me with a freedom of your own
And live and love and laugh so happily,
For life's short span can surely not condone,
Affairs of heart that emanate from darkly fear and selfish gain.

John Malcolm Stephen
16.II.67

John Stephen
1965

My Darling Margot,

Love me with a freedom of your own
And live and love and laugh so happily,
For life's short span can surely not condone,
Affairs of heart that emanate from darkly fear and selfish gain.

John Malcolm Stephen

16.II.67

121

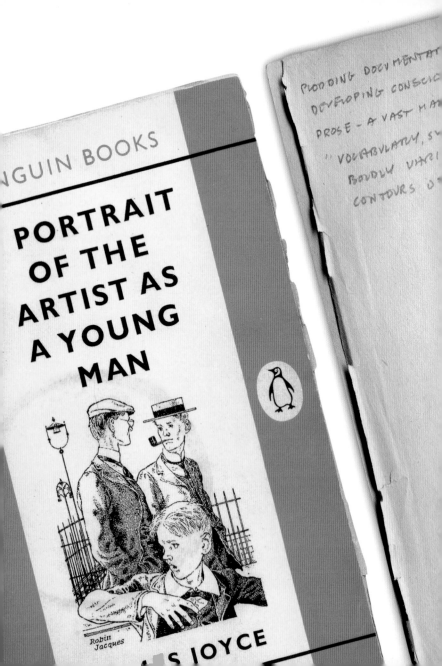

PENGUIN BOOKS
1477

A PORTRAIT OF THE ARTIST AS A YOUNG MAN

JAMES JOYCE

[handwritten annotations:]

HOES
RHYTHM ARE NOW
ACCENTUATE THE
UNDERLYING EMOTION."

Kyrilovitch
JAN. 1962.
Transfered to the
selves of Miss E. Pipes, in
deep gratitude for
her services to cultural
avancement.

£

Kyrilovitch
1 Jan, 1962.

Transferred to the selves of Miss E. Pipes, in deep
gratitude for her services to cultural advancement.

Plodding documentary.
Developing consciousness
Prose – a vast hall of echoes

"Vocabulary, syntax, rhythm are now boldly varied to
accentuate the contours of the underlying emotion."

Penguin Classics

FLAUBERT

SENTIMENTAL EDUCATION

THE PENGUIN CLASSICS
FOUNDER EDITOR (1944–64): E. V. RIEU
PRESENT EDITORS
Betty Radice and Robert Baldick
L 141

From one naughty young lady to another hoping that your mother doesn't know that you're out and that you wear only the best woolly bloomers

30.8.64.

on your quatercentenary

From one naughty young lady to another hoping that
your mother doesn't know that you're out and that
you wear only the best woolly bloomers.

30.8.64

on your quartercentury

JULES VERNE

TWENTY THOUSAND LEAGUES UNDER THE SEA

PENGUIN
POPULAR CLASSICS

Jan 2010

Ruby

In all the environments the world has to offer – from Canberra to London, above and below the water, – remember always that love actually manifests itself in so many wonderful ways.

Love, Indiana

Jan 2010
Ruby
In all the environments the world has to offer – from Canberra to
London, above and below the water, – remember always that love
actually manifests itself in so many wonderful ways.
Love, Indiana

THIS BOOK WAS
PUBLISHED IN 1949. IT
WAS ABOUT THE FUTURE 1984
    I HAVE GIVEN IT
TO YOU WITH LOVE IN
1994, THE START OF
    OUR FUTURE

[Signature]

This book was published in 1949 it was about the future 1984
I have given it to you with love in 1994, the start of our future

[Signature]

GEORGE ORWELL

NINETEEN EIGHTY-FOUR

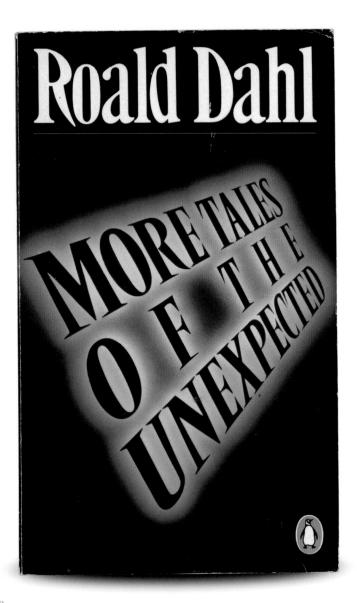

Roald Dahl

MORE TALES OF THE UNEXPECTED

Louise,
    You have given me so much.
I have only myself to give to you.
My Heart, My Soul and my body are
at your disposal.
dispose of carefully.

Mark

PENGUIN BO
MORE TAI

Roald Dahl's
in Llandaff,
Repton Scho
enlisted in t
wounded aft
later saw ser
In 1942 he we
and it was th
he was trans
as a Wing C
based on his
lished in lea
book, *Over*
ceived extrac
many langua
world. The
Someone Lik
Roald Dahl,
Anglia Telev
stories, which
Unexpected
other publica
Uncle Oswald
Best of Roald
The Collecte
volumes of a
tribute to Ro
published his

Roald Dahl

Louise,
You have given me so much. I have only myself to give to you.
My heart, my soul and my body are at your disposal.
dispose of carefully.
Mark

To Kim,
My love!
to the front
and the back of
your head!
to those long black
tresses
flowing down
shear summer dresses;
I see all and its
one vision, one vision
I alone own.
I am yours
always,

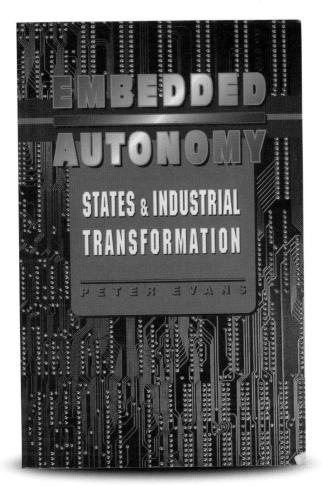

To Kim,
My love,
to the front and the back of your head,
to those long black tresses flowing down shear summer dresses;
I see all and it's one vision, one vision
I alone own.
I am yours
always
Stu

ORTON

The Complete Plays

ENTERTAINING MR SLOANE • LOOT

WHAT THE BUTLER SAW • THE RUFFIAN ON THE STAIR

THE ERPINGHAM CAMP • FUNERAL GAMES

THE GOOD AND FAITHFUL SERVANT

Introduced by John Lahr

Dear Neil,

"Lie on the couch with your hands behind your head & think of the closing chapters of your favourite work of fiction. The rest may be left to me"

Leaving me to say – enjoy every word & <u>don't</u> shut your eyes & don't think of England.

All my love, Naomi xx

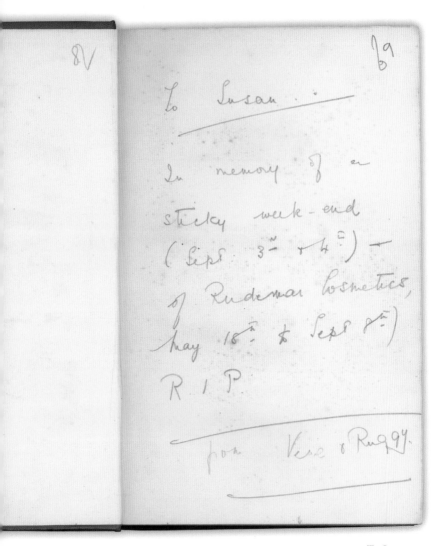

To Susan . . .

In memory of a sticky week-end (Sept 3rd & 4th) – of Ruderman Cosmetics, (May 18th to Sept 8th)

R I P.

from Vere & Ruggy

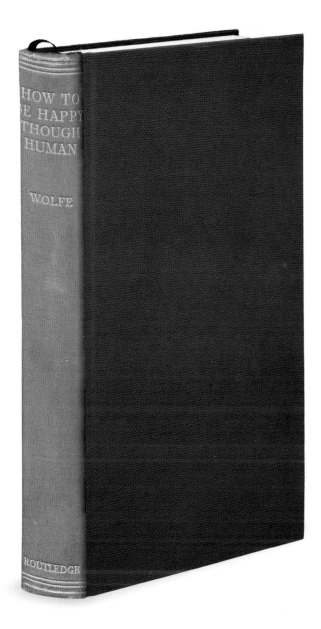

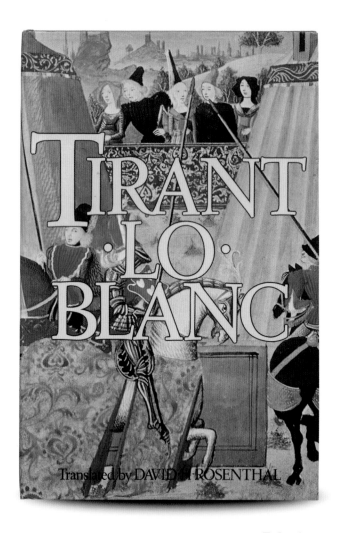

TIRANT ·LO· BLANC

Translated by DAVID H ROSENTHAL

To Jonathan,
All you need to know about being chivalrous, fighting dragons and
rescuing maidens or whatever the gay male equivalent of a maiden is.
Love and a kiss
David

December 1984

· for Stephanie Smolinsky ·

To Jonathan,
     All you need
to know about being
chivalrous, fighting
dragons and rescuing
maidens or whatever
the gay male equivalent
of a maiden is.
  Love and a Kiss
     David
      December 1984

From a selfish old slag
To a fat lazy old cow
Two years
?

140

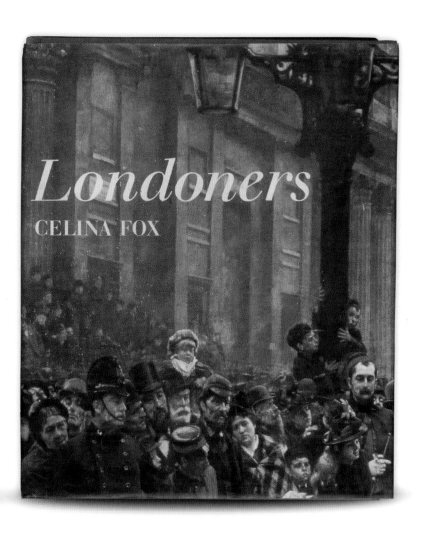

Londoners

CELINA FOX

To John Hughes.

Go shoot yourself.

Henry.

May 58

JUNGLE LORE
CORBETT
OXFORD

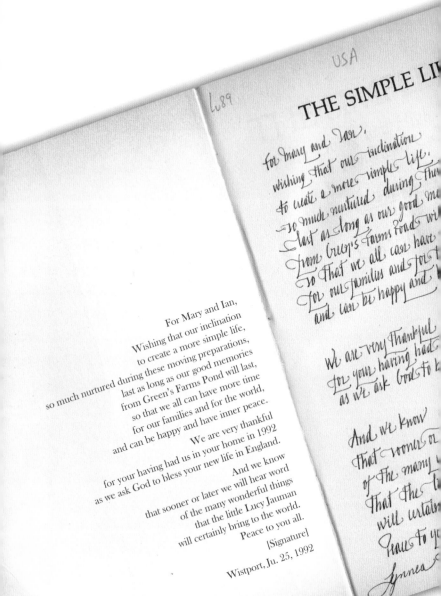

For Mary and Ian,
wishing that our inclination
to create a more simple life,
so much nurtured during Thu[...]
last as long as our good me[...]
from Green's Farms Pond wi[...]
so that we all can have [...]
for our families and for t[...]
and can be happy and [...]

We are very thankful
for your having had [...]
as we ask God to b[...]

And we know
that sooner o[...]
of the many [...]
that the t[...]
will certain[...]
Peace to yo[...]
Lynnea [...]

For Mary and Ian,
Wishing that our inclination
to create a more simple life,
so much nurtured during these moving preparations,
last as long as our good memories
from Green's Farms Pond will last,
so that we all can have more time
for our families and for the world,
and can be happy and have inner peace.

We are very thankful
for your having had us in your home in 1992
as we ask God to bless your new life in England.

And we know
that sooner or later we will hear word
of the many wonderful things
that the little Lucy Jauman
will certainly bring to the world.
Peace to you all.

[Signature]

Wistport, Ju. 25, 1992

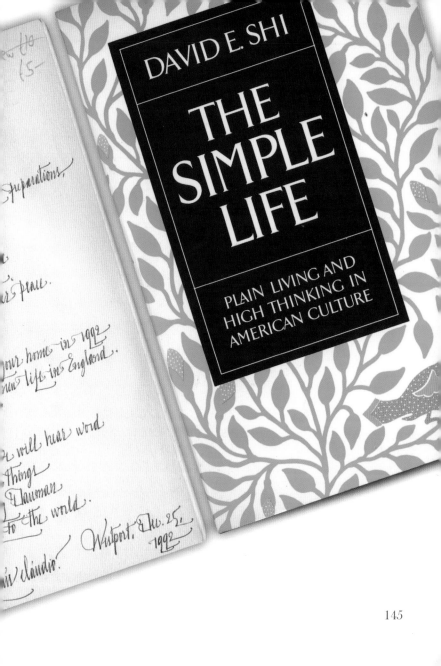

DAMON RUNYON

On Broadway

April 21st 97

To Peter

An also ran in the Afirkomen stakes at 6 to 5 improving to 7 to 3 –

"If laughter is a tonic then this book you will find to be a veritable elixir of life."

The odds are 100 to 1 or thereabouts that I will ever speak to you again should you lose, misplace, or otherwise fail to read this book from cover to cover and at the conclusion fail in the oral examination set by the "admirers of Damon Runyon society" since to pass the written test the odds are that you would need to improve your Yiddish spelling having seldom learnt to spell in English – amen. AP

Apr 21st 97

To Peter

An also ran in the
Afirkomen stakes
at 6 to 5
improving to 7 to 3

"If laughter is a tonic
then this book you will
find to be a veritible
elixir of life."

The odds are 100 to 1 or thereabouts
that I will ever speak to you
again should you lose, misplace, or
otherwise fail to read this book from
cover to cover and at the conclusion fail
in the oral examination set by the Admirers
of Damon Runyon society" since to pass the
written test the odds are that you would need
to improve your yiddish spelling having seldom
learnt to spell in English — amen.

HENRY
DAVID
THOREAU

COURAGE
CLASSICS

WALDEN

...er-

...enough
...ds for
...der-

...ry
...testing
...y escap-
...es and
...hoped to
...serious

...etailed ac-
...e shores of
...e a whole
...ees and cro...
...ns, all view...
...horeau's p...
...ntent to ob...
restless min... ...th...
he wrestled with the meaning o...
saw around him.
    Seeking solitude, Thoreau ...
tellectual freedom. While yo...
agree with all of the answers...
...loration will surely...
...wers of yo...

Dear Snell,
Happy birthday. Hope you enjoy this book, if you don't, send it
back and I'll never send you anything <u>ever again</u> oooh!
Spud. 2003.

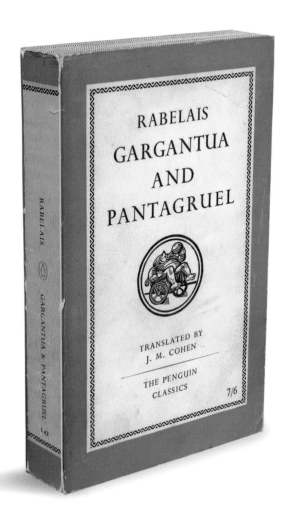

To Ken,

In the knowledge of your scatological tastes, with the realizations that you will never have time to read this (though I hope you will), and that you couldn't read it in the original if you wanted to, (and that for once is not an insult as old French is not everyone's forte).

"Mark, learn and inwardly digest"
— and please let me borrow it from time to time.

To Ken

In the knowledge of your
scatological tastes,
With the realization that
you will never have time
to read this (though I hope
you will), and that you
couldn't read it in the original
if you wanted to. (and that for
once is not an insult as Old
French is not everyone's forte).

"Mark, learn and inwardly digest"
— and please
let
me
borrow it from
time to time.

23/9/96

Sweetheart,

you are a darling and I love you but READ THE BOOK!

I desperately adore you and shall always look at you knowing this.

You are my wonderful world and my happy life.

Kisses forever,

Jodie.

23/9/96

Sweetheart,

you are a darling and I love you but **READ THE BOOK!**
I desperately adore you and shall always look at you knowing this.
You are my wonderful world and my happy life.

Kisses forever,

[Signature]

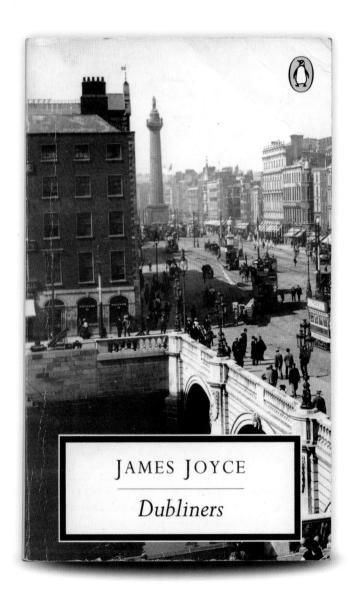

JAMES JOYCE

Dubliners

ONE IN TWENTY

A Study of
Homosexuality in Men and Women

BRYAN MAGEE

You leave this book alone, you filthy old man, who calls his wife "Mommie" and has "done it" with an African alyah!

LONDON
SECKER & WARBURG

You leave this book alone, you filthy old man, who calls his wife
'Mommie' and has 'done it' with an African alyah!

Bryan Magee • ONE IN TWENTY • Secker & Warburg

155

Conch from Enid, Christmas 1947.

'Wonder & wisdom belong to the country, criticism & knowledge to the town: and knowledge has small value compared with wisdom.' Sir William Beach Thomas

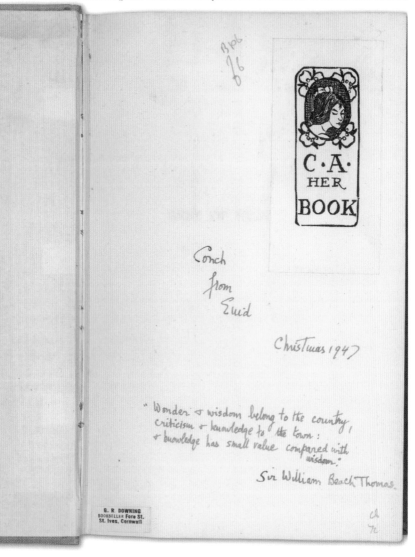

C·A·
HER
BOOK

Conch
from
Enid

Christmas 1947

" Wonder & wisdom belong to the country,
criticism & knowledge to the town:
& knowledge has small value compared with
wisdom."

Sir William Beach Thomas.

Owned by Stewart R. Valdar of Hampstead
Elementary my dear Watson . . .
Great Scott!
No . . . a genuine Stewie Valdar!
Love from Jean. Christmas 1972

SHERLOCK HOLMES
SHORT STORIES

A Conan Doyle

'I kept my answers small and kept them near;
Big questions bruised my mind but still I let
Small answers be a bulwark to my fear.

The huge abstractions I kept from the light;
Small things I handled and caressed and loved.
I let the stars assume the whole night.

But the big answers clamoured to be moved
Into my life. Their great audacity
Shouted to be acknowledged and believed.

Even when all small answers build up to
Protection of my spirit, still I hear
Big answers striving for their overthrow

And all the great conclusions coming near.

Happy Birthday, Christopher!
April 1989.

'I kept my answers small and kept them near;
Big questions bruised my mind but still I let
Small answers be a bulwark to my fear.
The huge abstractions I kept from the light;
Small things I handled and caressed and loved.
I let the stars assume the whole night.
But the big answers clamoured to be moved

Into my life. Their great audacity
Shouted to be acknowledged and believed.
Even when all small answers build up to
Protection of my spirit, still I hear
Big answers striving for their overthrow.
And all the great conclusions coming near.'

Happy Birthday, Christopher!
April 1989

THE
GOD OF
SMALL
THINGS

Sweetheart,

The God of Small Things
is the god of, well, the
everyday, the minutes spent
together that bind the day
to one another, the little
intimacies, things that others
forget, that we carry around
with us because that is who
we are and cannot get rid
of them, no matter hard
you wish or dry.

love,

THE GOD
OF
SMALL THINGS

A NOVEL

ARUNDHATI
ROY

Sweetheart,
The God of Small Things is the god of, well, the everyday, the minutes
spent together that bind the days to one another, the little intimacies, things
that others forget, that we carry around with us because that is who we are
and cannot get rid of them, no matter hard you wish or try.
Love [Signature]

From Justin to Rebecca,
With warm & tender feelings, on your birthday. £4

Gabriel García Márquez

19 August 2004

After rough seas, there is calm,
for sore wounds, there is a balm,

LOVE in the

Let me hold you in my arms

TIME of

and keep you safe from harm.

CHOLERA

TRANSLATED FROM THE SPANISH
BY EDITH GROSSMAN

PENGUIN BOOKS

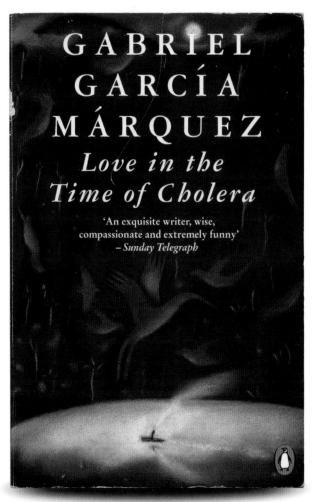

GABRIEL GARCÍA MÁRQUEZ

Love in the Time of Cholera

'An exquisite writer, wise,
compassionate and extremely funny'
– *Sunday Telegraph*

From Justin to Rebecca,
With warm & tender feelings on your birthday.
19 August 2004
After rough seas, there is calm,
for sore wounds, there is a balm.
Let me hold you in my arms
and keep you safe from harm.

WILLIAM BLAKE
Songs of Innocence

Color Facsimile of the First Edition with 31 Color Plates

London 19-5-1994

Toannandian & Isabellabella

ANNANDa is indian for joy

may youre life be filled
with annanda

May by the Grace
of the Divine
your lifes be
enlightened with
this joy

My heart will always
remember you and
be there for you
May peace be with you
all my love
Irene

London 19-5-1994
Toannandian & Isabellabella
Annanda is Indian for joy
May youre life be filled
with annanda
May by the Grace
of the Divine
your lifes be
enlightened with
this joy.

My heart will always
remember you and
be there for you
May peace be with you.
All my love
Ireue

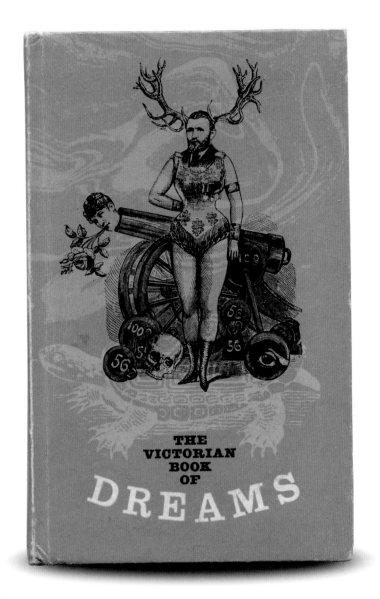

THE
VICTORIAN
BOOK
OF
DREAMS

for Stevie, the man who this book was surely written for, and who has perhaps a mole on either ankle — to wish you a happy birthday, and dreams full of mackerel and devoid of pantomime.

with love,

Lea x

For Stevie, the man who this book was surely written for, and who has perhaps a mole on either ankle – to wish you a happy birthday, and dreams full of mackerel and devoid of pantomime.
With love,
Lea x

[See author note p185]

CARSON McCULLERS

THE MEMBER
OF THE WEDDING

[handwritten inscription:]

Happy Valentine's Day, Sue.

February 14th year 1973

Good friend.

Everyone wants to
belong ... to others

your dear american
friend & sister

faith.

much love.

THE M

Carson
Georgia,
Fellow
also rece
Academ
wrote T
Reflectio
ber of th
New Yo
staged a
The Bal
Root of
Without
and Clea
was a F
Arts and

Happy Valentine's Day, Sue
February 14th year 1973
Good friend.
Everyone wants to belong . . . to others [heart doodle]
Your dear american friend & sister
Faith.
Much love. [heart doodle]

Deb,

Just a little book full of words appropriate for your . . .

"desperately excited and very happy" state of being!!

With much love, big smiles and a few tears . . .

Nicola
xx

Deb,
Just a little book full of words
appropriate for your . . .
"desperately excited and
very happy"
state of being!!
With much love, big smiles
and a few tears . . .
Nicola
xx

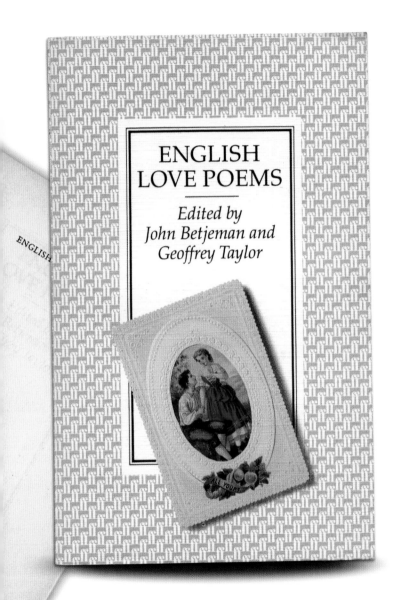

ENGLISH
LOVE POEMS

Edited by
John Betjeman and
Geoffrey Taylor

to Chiko,
with love Mark xx.

LUX THE POET

Martin Miller

'cause I thought that
maybe my baby would
like it. My wonderful love, Bulman,
And i was just thinking today
sipping latte in Brick Lane that
my heart cries for you. I love you
more and more. I'm yours as a
poet, as a woman, as a wandering
Jew who found home...

XXXX XXX

Your
FOURTH ESTATE · London
DIMENSION LOVER

LU^x the POET

M a r t i n   M i l l a r

'BRITAIN'S FUNNIEST NEW WRITER' THE FACE

To Ch[. . .], with love M[. . .]

'Cause I thought that maybe my baby would like it. My wonderful love,
Bulmau. And I was just thinking today sipping latte in Brick Lane that
my heart longs for you. I love you more and more I'm yours as a poet,
as a woman, as a wandering Jew who found a home . . .

xxxxxxx

Your Fourth Dimension Lover

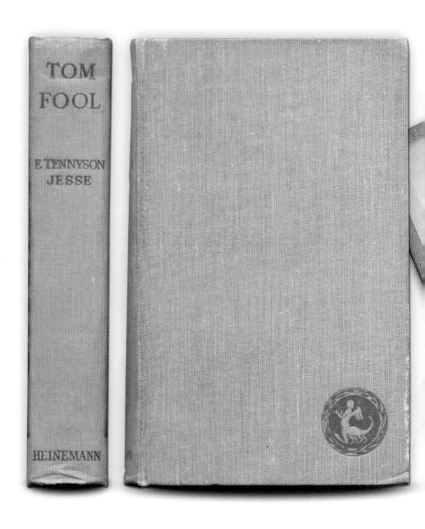

To my Stiffy,
In remembrance of the anniversary of the most important day in my life.
From his Slutty

March 19th 1928

To my Stiffy

In remembrance of
the anniversary of
the most important
day in my life.

from his Shorty

March 19th 1928

Worzel Gummidge

Barbara Euphan Todd

A Puffin Book 3/6

£2

. . . .

If this book should ever roam,
box its ears and send it home

. . . .

May 1991

Dear John,

When I was twelve or thirteen years old Grandma became increasingly alarmed at my philistine preoccupation with science and agriculture. I remember being whisked off to the bookshop in Bury, where on my behalf she selected "Mister Johnson", my first 'adult' book.

It was an inspired choice – it amused me, introduced me to the joys of literature and also to the notion of an overseas colonial service. The book thus had a profound influence on my life; without it I may never have gone to Africa, and you may not have been born thirty years ago. To it you probably owe your existence and it is high time you were introduced. I pass it to you in turn with much love.

Dad

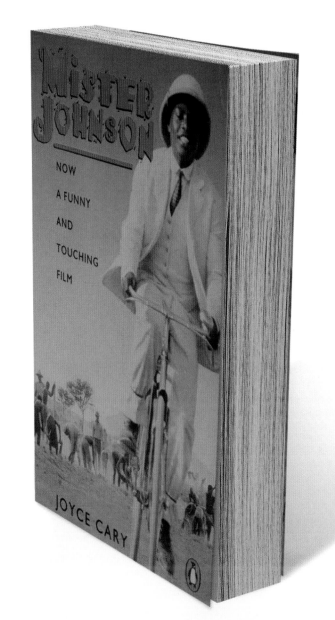

MISTER JOHNSON

NOW

A FUNNY

AND

TOUCHING

FILM

JOYCE CARY

I love you.
x x x

Author Notes

PP 54 and 55
29 September 1938 saw the signing of the Munich Agreement.

PP 84 and 85
This edition of Peter Pan was published in 2010.

PP 98 and 99
'Every Little Bit Hurts' was written by Ed Cobb and was originally a hit single for Motown singer Brenda Holloway in 1964. *The Cold Embrace* is an anthology of macabre short stories by women writers, published in 1966.

PP 168 and 169
Mackerel – Dreaming that you see these fishes in the water is good, denoting success in trade, prosperity and good fortune to the dreamer. If you dream of stinking mackerel, you will never marry you present sweetheart.'
'Pantomime – To dream of witnessing a pantomime signifies low pursuits; if you enter, after this dream, upon a theatrical profession, it will be without honour, and you will end life
an outcast.'
'A mole on either ankle denotes a man to be inclined to effeminacy and elegancy of dress . . .'
Taken from *The Victorian Book of Dreams*.

Copyright Information

The following covers reproduced by kind permission of Penguin Books:

A Time of Gifts by Patrick Leigh Fermor (1988)
Cannery Row by John Steinbeck (1994)
The Prime of Miss Jean Brodie by Muriel Spark (1969)
The Princess and the Goblin by George McDonald (1967)
One Day in the Life of Ivan Denisovich by Alexander Solzhenitsyn (1971)
Words by Jean-Paul Sartre (1972)
Animal Farm by George Orwell (1971)
The Penguin Book of Infidelities, edited by Stephen Brook (1995)
Selected Modern Short Stories, edited by Alan Steele (1938)
Piers the Plowman by William Langland (1982)
I, Claudius by Robert Graves (1964)
Peter Pan by J.M. Barrie (2010)
The Three Hostages by John Buchan (1955)
Three Men in a Boat by Jerome K. Jerome (1994)
Decline and Fall by Evelyn Waugh (1987)
The Beautiful and the Damned by F. Scott Fitzgerald (??)
A Severed Head by Iris Murdoch (1964)
Three Guineas by Viriginia Woolf (1977)
A Portrait of the Artist as a Young Man by James Joyce (1960)
Sentimental Education by Gustave Flaubert (1964)
Twenty Thousand Leagues Under the Sea by Jules Verne (1994)
Nineteen Eighty-Four by George Orwell (1990)
More Tales of the Unexpected by Roald Dahl (1980)
On Broadway by Damon Runyon (1990)
Gargantua and Pantagruel by Francois Rabelais(1957)
Dubliners by James Joyce (1992)
Fruits of the Earth by André Gide (1988)
Love in the Time of Cholera by Gabriel García Márquez (1985, 1988)
Worzel Gummidge by Barbara Euphan Todd (1965)
Mister Johnson by Joyce Cary (1991)
The Member of the Wedding by Carson McCullers (1972)

The following covers reproduced by kind permission of HarperCollins Publishers Ltd:

Winner Take Nothing ©1939 Ernest Hemingway
Papillon ©1969 Henri Charrière
Death on the Nile ©1937 Agatha Christie
Lux the Poet ©1988 Martin Millar
Unemployment and Plenty ©1933 Shipley N. Brayshaw

The following covers used by permission of the Random House Group Limited:

Literate Passion – Letters of Anais Nin and Henry Miller, published by WH Allen and Co.

The Swimming Pool Library by Alan Hollingsurst, published by Vintage

The Cold Embrace edited by Alex Hamilton, published by Corgi

Tom Fool by F. Tennyson Jesse published by William Heinemann

The following covers reproduced by permission of Random House Inc:

The God of Small Things. Book cover © 1997 by Random House LLC; from *The God of Small Things* by Arundhati Roy. Used by permission of Random House, an imprint of the Random House Publishing Group, a division of Random House LLC. All rights reserved.

Letter to a Christian Nation. Book cover © 2008 by Vintage Books, an imprint of Random House LLC; from Letter to a Christian Nation by Sam Harris. Used by permission of Alfred A. Knopf, an imprint of the Knopf Doubleday Publishing Group, a division of Random House LLC. All rights reserved.

The Arabian Nights – Tales from A Thousand and One Nights. Book cover, copyright © 1997 by Random House LLC; from The Arabian Nights by Richard Burton. Used by permission of Modern Library, an imprint of The Random House Publishing Group, a division of Random House LLC. All rights reserved.

Bawdy Ballads reproduced by kind permission of Omnibus Press

Much Ado About Nothing by William Shakespeare reproduced by kind permission of Dover Publications, New York.

Thanks to

_____

Terry Mitson at Spitalfields Market, London.

Chris Edwards and all the staff at Skoob Books,
Marchmount Street, London.

Merissa Fuentes at the British Heart Foundation,
Holloway Road, London.

Jen Wilkinson at Bookmarks, Bloomsbury
Street, London.

Katy Stoddard at Oxfam Books, Muswell Hill,
London, all the staff at Oxfam Books, Upper
Street & Bloomsbury Street branches and
Stafford and Mark Crombie at Stafford's Gallery,
Charing Cross Road.

Anthony Smith and Jennie Patterson at Slightly
Foxed.

And also thanks to Pete Brown, David
Clack, Sarah Crown, Brian & Carol & Marc
Gooderham, Sophie Lambert, Leanne Oliver,
Polly Osborn, David Owen, Miriam Robinson,
Michelle Signore, Liz Vater.

http://bookdedications.wordpress.com

The End